# The Anglican Evangelical Doctrine of Infant Baptism

BY JOHN STOTT & J. ALEC MOTYER

*The Latimer Trust*

© J R W Stott 2008 and J A Motyer 2008

ISBN   978 0 946307 96 8

Cover photo: *Happy baby girl* © travis manley – fotolia.com

Published by the Latimer Trust

PO Box 26685

London N14 4XQ

www.latimertrust.org

# CONTENTS

*Preface* by *Lee Gatiss* ................................................................1

*The Evangelical Doctrine of Baptism* by *John Stott* ................5

1. *The Meaning of Baptism* ...............................................7

2. *The Effect of Baptism* ..................................................10

3. *Conclusion*.....................................................................20

*Baptism in the Book of Common Prayer* by *Alec Motyer*.......23

1. *The Unity of Baptism and the Lord's Supper in One Identical Sacramental Principle*..................................26

2. *The Association between Regeneration and Baptism*....33

3. *The Identity of Meaning between Adult and Infant Baptism* ......................................................................42

# Preface

Why publish together these two papers on the Anglican Evangelical doctrine of infant baptism? First, there is still relatively little written from an Anglican Evangelical viewpoint on the subject of infant (or paedo) baptism. We remain grateful to Michael Green for a helpful chapter on the subject in his little book, *Baptism: It's Purpose, Practice and Power* (first published in 1987), yet it is a pity not to see this joined on the bookshelves by many other volumes from evangelicals on this controversial and sometimes perplexing subject. Baptism is of course one of those subjects on which we have obvious differences with many of our closest friends and gospel partners in non-Anglican evangelical churches. So perhaps a certain reticence to discuss this potentially divisive 'distinctive' is therefore understandable. Yet secondary issues are not unimportant issues, and with care it should be possible robustly to expound a view on such matters while graciously maintaining fellowship with brothers and sisters who read the Scriptures differently at this point.

Second, there is some confusion regarding baptism in a number of our churches at present, with many lapsing into a kind of default anti-paedobaptism (sometimes misleadingly called credobaptism, as if Anglicans did not also baptize adult converts!). This mystification in the pews may be due partly to the absence of seemingly trustworthy material on the subject. There are many Presbyterian works of great value, clarity, and erudition, but less from a distinctively Anglican perspective that is dependable. Our modern liturgies are often deliberately ambiguous and usually left unexplained, while few expository preachers would pause in a standard Sunday sermon to unpack the implications of their text for the doctrine of infant baptism. It is to be feared, therefore, that congregations are not often exposed to the biblical and theological reasoning behind the practice, which leaves them only with superstitious or erroneous explanations from less reliable sources that can quickly be dismissed by the biblically literate. It may also be that uncertainty in the pews is due to uncertainty in the pastor's study.

In the light of these two considerations then, to continue publishing solid teaching in this area is vital for thinking laypeople, ministers, and especially ordinands, some of whom will not have come to settled convictions regarding the propriety of baptizing infants prior to being accepted for training.

Furthermore, there are movements within Reformed and conservative evangelicalism at present, with support from certain circles in the United States, which are strongly and passionately paedobaptist but which also defend some less mainstream evangelical views. 'Federal Vision' theology, for example, has proved to be somewhat divisive and controversial in some quarters, as has the so-called 'New Perspective'. Yet it would be a mistake to so associate a belief in infant baptism with the Federal Vision that holding to the former was thought to implicate every paedobaptist in the perceived peculiarities of the latter (be it post-millennialism, preterism, or paedocommunion). Some critics can see a Romanizing 'high church' drift or an American home-schooling conspiracy behind everyone who holds convictions regarding infant baptism (even just standard Anglican convictions)!

It is refreshing then, in such a context, to read again the following papers by two fine scholar-pastors of unimpeachably evangelical credentials. John R. W. Stott CBE is Rector Emeritus of All Souls, Langham Place in London and over the last 60 years has been one of the most influential leaders of evangelicalism worldwide. J. Alec Motyer is the former Principal of Trinity College, Bristol, and was for many years incumbent of St. Luke's, West Hampstead and later minister of Christ Church, Westbourne. Both have been awarded a Lambeth D.D. for their scholarly contributions to the church and are respectively the New Testament and Old Testament Editors of the widely-acclaimed *Bible Speaks Today* series of evangelical commentaries. Their reputations were not gained by importing the traditional frameworks of systematic categories onto Scripture but through rigorous devotion to the hard work of exegesis in the context of the whole Bible, which is the hallmark of all truly evangelical hermeneutics.

In what follows, Drs. Stott and Motyer defend biblically the doctrine of infant baptism and its proper evangelical practice within the Church of England. Since these papers were originally written well before any current furore they demonstrate effectively that covenantal infant baptism is a reliably evangelical and Anglican view to hold, and has been for quite some time. Whilst they may not answer directly more recent arguments that have been brought against infant baptism, they certainly do set out (in a characteristically lucid fashion) the broad parameters of the traditional Anglican Evangelical approach. There may be other approaches to defending the truth of infant baptism, and alternative ways of understanding the texts, which still reach the same ultimate conclusions. More recent discussions may at times provide more compelling syntheses. But Stott and Motyer speak to reassure a new generation of Anglican Evangelical paedobaptists that theirs is no new or peculiar doctrine, and to persuade those who may not have fully appreciated the Reformed heritage we in the Church of England enjoy.

I am grateful to the authors for their kind permission to reproduce these articles which were both originally published elsewhere. I have indulged in only light editing of the text for the sake of readability (e.g. removing capital letters from pronouns referring to God), and in Dr. Motyer's chapter I have substituted the English Standard Version for the original Authorised Version in quotations from the Bible. I am delighted to commend these expositions to a new and wider audience, conscious of these wise and inspiring words from the great Anglican Evangelical, J. C. Ryle:

> The subject of infant baptism is undoubtedly a delicate and difficult one. Holy and praying men are unable to see alike upon it. Although they read the same Bible, and profess to be led by the same Spirit, they arrive at different

conclusions about this sacrament. The great majority of Christians hold, that infant baptism is Scriptural and right. A comparatively small section of the Protestant Church, but one containing many eminent saints among its members, regards infant baptism as unscriptural and wrong... But the difference now referred to, must not make members of the Church of England shrink from holding decided opinions on the subject. That church has declared plainly in its Articles that 'the baptism of young children is in any wise to be retained, as most agreeable with the institution of Christ.' To this opinion we need not be afraid to adhere.[1]

May this small book go some way towards helping us as Anglican Evangelicals to recover that same gracious yet unashamed confidence.


LEE GATISS

LONDON

---

[1] J. C. Ryle, *Expository Thoughts on Mark* (Edinburgh: Banner of Truth, 1985), page 204.

# The Evangelical Doctrine of Baptism

by John Stott

| | | |
|---|---|---|
| 1. | The Meaning of Baptism | 7 |
| 1.1. | Baptism signifies union with Christ | 7 |
| 1.2. | Baptism signifies the forgiveness of sins | 8 |
| 1.3. | Baptism signifies the gift of the Spirit | 8 |
| 2. | The Effect of Baptism | 10 |
| 2.1. | The ex opere operato view | 11 |
| 2.2. | The Bare Token view. | 15 |
| 2.3. | The Covenant Sign view. | 15 |
| 3. | Conclusion | 20 |
| 3.1. | The doctrine of assurance | 20 |
| 3.2. | The discipline of baptism. | 20 |
| 3.3. | The practice of evangelism. | 22 |

# The Evangelical Doctrine of Baptism

Let me introduce this subject with two preliminary statements:

(i) *Evangelical churchmen do not treat the sacrament of baptism lightly.* We do not forget that it was instituted by the risen Lord, nor that it was administered by the infant Church from the Day of Pentecost onwards (Acts 2:38, 41). Because of the precept of Christ and the practice of the apostles, it is the plain duty of every professing Christian to ask for baptism for himself and his children; and of the ordained minister to press upon his congregation this obligation and privilege.

(ii) It is the claim of the evangelical churchman that his doctrine of baptism is *the biblical doctrine.* At all events, he could not contemplate the existence of an *evangelical* doctrine of baptism as distinct from a *biblical* doctrine; since his primary concern is to understand the biblical doctrine and to conform his thinking and practice to it. If the so-called 'evangelical' doctrine of baptism can be shown to be unbiblical, the evangelical churchman is ready to abandon it in favour of any doctrine which can be shown to be more biblical.

My task then is first to seek to establish the biblical doctrine of baptism, and secondly, to show that the teaching of *The Book of Common Prayer* and the Articles can and should be interpreted in a way that is fully consistent with the biblical doctrine.

In this study I am *not* concerned with the proper *mode* of baptism (whether by affusion or immersion), nor with the proper *subjects* for baptism (whether adults and infants, or adults only); but rather with the meaning and the effect of the sacrament, that is, what it signifies and how it operates.

# 1.    The Meaning of Baptism

The best way to introduce the meaning of baptism is to assert that both the sacraments of the gospel are essentially sacraments of *grace*, that is, sacraments of divine initiative, not of human activity. The clearest evidence of this in the case of baptism is that, in the New Testament, the candidate never baptizes himself, but always submits to being baptized by another. In his baptism, he is a passive recipient of something that is done to him. The Articles are quite clear about this. For instance, Articles twenty-five, twenty-seven and twenty-eight all begin with the statement that a sacrament is a sign not of what we do or are, but of what God has done, or does.

Now, granted that baptism is a sacrament of grace, what grace of God does it signify? The answer to this question is threefold.

## 1.1.    *Baptism signifies union with Christ*

God's chief grace to undeserving sinners is his plan to unite them to his Son. That this is the primary meaning of baptism is clear from the use of the [Greek] preposition *eis* with the verb 'to baptize'. Just as the passage of the Red Sea was a baptism *eis* (into) Moses (1 Corinthians 10:2), so Christian baptism is baptism not into any man (1 Corinthians 1:13) but into Christ (Romans 6:3). It is true that sometimes baptism is said to be *en* or *epi* the name of Christ (Acts 10:48; 2:38), but the commonest preposition is *eis*, 'into the name of the Lord Jesus' (Acts 8:16; 19:5).

It is true again that, according to the Matthaean record of the institution of baptism, baptism was to be into the one name of the three Persons of the Trinity (Matthew 28:19), but this gives place in Acts and the Epistles to baptism into the name of Jesus – probably because it is he who revealed the Father and sent the Holy Spirit, so that we cannot be related to him without being related to them also.

Further, baptism into the name of Christ is baptism into Christ crucified and risen (Romans 6:3, 4). This union with Christ crucified and risen signifies participation in the virtue of his death and the power of his resurrection, the end (by death or burial) of the old life of sin, and the beginning (by resurrection or rebirth) of the new life of righteousness. This union with Christ in his death and resurrection, and the beginning of a new life, is the controlling idea in baptism, and the next two meanings simply amplify the benefit of sharing in the death and resurrection of Christ.

## 1.2.  *Baptism signifies the forgiveness of sins*

It is safe to say that all religious water rituals are purification ceremonies, and Christian baptism is no exception. 'Repent and be baptized every one of you in the name of Jesus Christ for the forgiveness of your sins', said Peter on the Day of Pentecost (Acts 2:38). 'Rise, and be baptized, and wash away your sins, calling on his name', said Ananias to Paul (Acts 22:16). Similarly, it is almost certain that the phrases 'but you were washed' (1 Corinthians 6:11), and 'the washing of regeneration' (Titus 3:5) are references to baptism. The washing of our bodies with pure water (Hebrews 10:22) signifies the washing of the soul from the defilement of sin.

## 1.3.  *Baptism signifies the gift of the Spirit*

It is well known that John the Baptist (according to the four evangelists) contrasted his own water-baptism with the Spirit-baptism which the Messiah would administer: 'I baptize you with water... He will baptize you with the Holy Spirit' (Matthew 3:11). In view of this contrast, we would expect that when Jesus Christ began to baptize with the Spirit, all baptism with water would cease. The fact that water-baptism continued, by special command of the risen Christ, suggests that it now intended to signify the very Spirit-baptism with which it had previously been contrasted. The pouring of water by which we receive the baptism of water, dramatizes the outpouring of the Spirit by which we receive the baptism of the Spirit. Peter seems to have understood this on the Day of

8

Pentecost, for, having interpreted the coming of the Spirit as the fulfilment of God's promise to pour out his Spirit on all flesh, he said: 'Repent and be baptized every one of you in the name of Jesus Christ for the forgiveness of your sins; and you shall receive the gift of the Holy Spirit. For the promise is to you and to your children, and to all that are far off, every one whom the Lord our God calls to him' (Acts 2:38, 39). Here baptism is associated with both the forgiveness of sins and the gift of the Spirit.

These two blessings were distinctive blessings of the New Covenant promised by God through the prophets. Baptism is therefore to be understood as an eschatological sacrament, inasmuch as it initiates into the New Covenant which belongs to the New Age. It does this by incorporating us *into Christ*, for Jesus Christ is the mediator of the New Covenant, and the bestower of its blessings.

To sum up, baptism signifies union with Jesus Christ in his death and resurrection, involving the end of the old life (through the forgiveness of sins) and the beginning of a new life (through the gift of the Spirit). Alternatively, baptism signifies union with Christ bringing both justification (a once for all cleansing and acceptance) and regeneration (a new birth by the Spirit unto a life of righteousness). To these three meanings of baptism we must add that incorporation into Christ includes incorporation into the Body of Christ, the Church.

With all this *The Book of Common Prayer* is fully consistent:

*(i) Union with Christ.* In the Catechism, the second answer declares that in baptism 'I was made a member of Christ'. This is the controlling idea – incorporation into Christ. Such a union with Christ involves 'a death unto sin and a new birth unto righteousness' through becoming partakers of Christ's death and resurrection.

*(ii) Forgiveness.* Familiar expressions in the Baptism Service are 'the everlasting benediction of thy heavenly washing',

and 'the mystical washing away of sin'.

*(iii) The Gift of the Spirit.* 'Regeneration by thy Holy Spirit' is the gift signified in baptism for which we give thanks.

These two blessings are brought together in Article twenty-seven: 'the promises of the forgiveness of sins and of our adoption to be the sons of God by the Holy Ghost are visibly signed and sealed'.

(iv) *Church membership.* The service speaks of a reception, grafting, or incorporation into Christ's holy Church, or the congregation of Christ's flock.

We turn now from the meaning of baptism to its effect; from what it signifies to how it operates.


2.　　*The Effect of Baptism*

We would all (I imagine) agree with the definition of a sacrament given in the Catechism: 'an outward and visible sign of an inward and spiritual grace given unto us, as a means whereby we receive the same, and a pledge to assure us thereof'.

So far we have been seeking to define the inward and spiritual grace of which baptism is the outward and visible sign. We now go on to define the relation between the visible sacrament and the invisible grace, between the sign and the thing signified, and thus to define the effect or operation of the sacrament.

Three main views have been held. The first is the view that the sign always conveys the gift, automatically, by itself, *ex opere operato,* so that all those who receive the sign willy-nilly also receive the thing signified.

The second is the view (at the opposite extreme) that the sign effects precisely nothing. It *signifies* the gift visibly, but in no sense or circumstance *conveys* it. It is a bare token or symbol, and that is all. Neither of these is the evangelical doctrine of baptism.

The third and evangelical view is that the sign not only signifies the gift, but seals or pledges it, and pledges it in such a way as to convey not indeed the gift itself, but a title to the gift – the baptized person receiving the gift (thus pledged to him) *by faith,* which may be before, during or after the administration of the sacrament.

The best way to proceed will be to examine these three views consecutively – the *ex opere operato* view, the bare token view, and the covenant sign view.

## 2.1.    *The ex opere operato view*

This is the view that the sign always, inevitably and unconditionally conveys the thing signified, through the power of the sacrament itself, or of God's promise attached to the sacrament. The consequence of this view is to suppose that all baptized persons (especially infants) are regenerate.

Apart from the *pragmatic* argument that all baptized persons do not *seem* to be regenerate, for they do not supply evidence of their regeneration in a life of godliness and holiness, there are two strong *biblical arguments* against this view. They concern the nature of the Church, and the way of salvation.

### 2.1.1.    *The nature of the Church.*

However unfashionable it may be today, the Bible does envisage a difference between the visible and the invisible Church. We do not mean by this that a person can belong to the invisible Church without responsible membership of a local, visible manifestation of it, but rather that it is possible to belong to a visible church without belonging to the true Church, the Body of Christ, which is invisible in the sense that its members are known to God alone (2 Timothy 2:19).

As St Augustine wrote: 'Many of those within are without; and some of those without are within'. Again, Bishop John

Pearson, in his famous *An Exposition of the Creed* wrote: 'I conclude therefore, as the ancient Catholicks did against the Donatists, that within the Church, in the public profession and external communion thereof, are contained persons truly good and sanctified, and hereafter saved, and together with them other persons void of all saving grace, and hereafter to be damned.'

Thus, St John writes of certain heretics that 'they went out from us, but they were not of us...' (1 John 2:19). They were members (doubtless baptized members), but though 'with us' outwardly and visibly, they were not 'of us', not genuine, but spurious.

Similarly, Paul writes at the beginning of 1 Corinthians 10 of the Old Testament Church in the wilderness 'that our fathers were all... baptized into Moses in the cloud and in the sea, and all ate the same spiritual food and all drank the same spiritual drink... Nevertheless with most of them God was not pleased; for they were overthrown in the wilderness.' The apostle deliberately describes them as baptized communicants, who nevertheless were overthrown in the wilderness; which shows that baptized communicant membership of the church is no guarantee of salvation.

The significance of this distinction between the visible and the invisible Church is that the visible Church consists of the baptized, while the invisible Church consists of the regenerate. Since the two companies are not identical, not all the baptized are regenerate.

Simon Magus is an example. He professed faith, was baptized, and no doubt passed as a church member, but Peter described him as being yet 'in the gall of bitterness and in the bond of iniquity', with his 'heart not right in the sight of God' (Acts 8: 13-24).

If Paul could write 'he is not a real Jew who is one outwardly, nor is true circumcision something external and physical. He is a Jew who is one inwardly, and real circumcision is a matter of the heart, spiritual and not literal', we could say the same of the Christian and baptism (Romans 2:28, 29).

## 2.1.2. *The way of salvation.*

Salvation is variously described in the New Testament, but we have already seen that two of its constituent parts are justification and regeneration. One is a legal, the other a biological metaphor, but they are two sides of the same coin. It is impossible to be regenerate without being justified.

Over and over again the New Testament writers declare that we are justified by faith, or (more accurately) by grace through faith. It is impossible to reconcile this doctrine with the view that justification is by grace through baptism, with or without faith. If faith is necessary for salvation, then the unbelieving candidate is not saved through baptism. What Paul writes in Romans 6 about being baptized into Christ must not be interpreted in such a way that it contradicts his teaching in chapters three to five of the same epistle, that we are justified by faith.

Various attempts have been made to reconcile the doctrines of baptismal regeneration and justification by faith – mainly by diluting the meaning either of the regeneration of which baptism is the sacrament, or of the faith through which sinners are justified.

Thus, some of the schoolmen taught that if the necessary qualification for baptism in adults was repentance and faith, its equivalent in infants was simply their infantine condition; that is, the full-orbed saving faith of the New Testament was not necessary in their case.

Luther (followed by other Reformers) attempted a reconciliation by asserting that God by his word actually implants faith in infants to qualify them for baptism.

Others have tried to retain both baptismal regeneration and justification by faith by diluting the content not of faith but of regeneration. They debase it from the inward new birth unto righteousness (which it always means in the New Testament) into an admission to the external privileges of the Covenant; or into an implanted capacity or faculty which does not necessarily issue in good works, i.e. a goodness which is potential rather than actual; or into merely the negative remission of original sin (as Augustine, and some Calvinists). But there is no biblical warrant for this eviscerated idea of regeneration, which in Scripture always means a supernatural birth effected by the Holy Spirit and manifest in holy living.

These attempts to reconcile baptismal regeneration and justification by faith are unsuccessful because we have no right to give to either regeneration or faith any meaning less than their full biblical meaning. Therefore if a sinner is justified by God through faith alone, he is not regenerate through baptism without faith.

Turning to the Articles, we find their teaching consistent with the rejection of the *ex opere operato* view of baptism, namely their insistence that the efficacy of the sacraments is dependent on worthy reception. At the end of Article twenty-five there is the general statement that 'in such only as worthily receive the same they have a wholesome effect or operation...' Similarly, in Article twenty-seven, it is 'they that receive baptism *rightly'* who are grafted into the Church, and to whom God's promises are visibly signed and sealed.

If we ask what is meant by a 'right' or 'worthy' reception, Article twenty-eight explains 'insomuch that to such as rightly, worthily *and with faith* receive the same, the Bread which we break is a partaking of the Body of Christ...' A right and worthy reception of the sacraments is a *believing* reception; without faith the sacraments have no wholesome operation or effect; rather the reverse.

The Catechism similarly lays emphasis on the necessary conditions required of candidates for baptism, and other statements in the Cathechism which may be thought to support the *ex opere operato* view must be understood in the light of these conditions.

The benefits of baptism are not bestowed unconditionally, they are appropriated by faith. Unworthy reception brings not blessing but judgment.

To quote the Gorham Judgment: 'That baptism is a sacrament generally necessary to salvation, but that the grace of regeneration does not so necessarily accompany the act of baptism that regeneration invariably takes place in baptism; that the grace may be granted before, in, or after baptism; that baptism is an effectual sign of grace by which God works invisibly in us, but only in such as worthily receive it – in them alone it has a wholesome effect; and that without reference to the qualification of the recipient it is not in itself an effectual sign of grace; that infants baptized and dying before actual sin are undoubtedly saved, but that in no case is baptism unconditional.'

## 2.2.    *The Bare Token view.*

I think I can dismiss this view in a sentence or two. If baptism were a mere sign, which in no sense or circumstance whatever conveyed anything to its recipients, the apostles could never have used expressions which ascribe some effect to baptism like 'repent and be baptized for the remission of sins' (Acts 2:38), or 'as many of you as were baptized into Christ have put on Christ' (Galatians 3:27), or 'baptism now saves you' (1 Peter 3:21). In what sense these expressions should be interpreted we will discuss later; for the moment it is enough that they demolish the notion that baptism's function is merely to *signify* grace and not in any sense to *convey* it.

## 2.3.    *The Covenant Sign view.*

The evangelical (or 'reformed') view of baptism is founded upon God's covenant of grace, and regards baptism as essentially the God-appointed sign which *seals* the blessings of the covenant to the individual Christian believer.

Pierre Marcel writes that 'the doctrine of the Covenant is

the germ, the root, the pith of all revelation, and consequently of all theology; it is the clue to the whole history of redemption'.[2] Hooker wrote that 'baptism implieth a covenant or league between God and man'.[3] I cannot stop to argue that the so-called New Covenant (mediated by Jesus and ratified by his blood) was *new* only in relation to the Covenant of Sinai. In itself it was not New (as Paul argues in Galatians), but the fulfillment of God's covenant with Abraham, so that those who are Christ's are Abraham's seed, heirs according to promise (Galatians 3:29).

To quote Calvin, 'the covenant is the same, the reason for confirming it is the same. Only the mode of confirming is different; for to them it was confirmed by circumcision, which among us is succeeded by baptism.'[4] That is, baptism has replaced circumcision as the covenant sign.

If this is so, and the place held by circumcision in the covenant in Abraham's day is occupied by baptism in the covenant in our day, what is this? The place and function of circumcision is defined in Romans 4:11, where Abraham is said to have 'received circumcision as a sign or seal of the righteousness which he had by faith while he was still uncircumcised'. Here it is said that Abraham received two gifts. First, he received justification, acceptance, by faith, while still uncircumcised. Secondly, he received circumcision as a sign and seal of this righteousness. The righteousness was given him in Genesis 15; its seal in Genesis 17. Now, what circumcision was to Abraham, Isaac and his descendants, baptism is to us. It is not only the sign of covenant membership, but a seal or pledge of covenant blessings. Baptism does not convey these blessings to us, but conveys to us a right or title to them, so that if and when we truly believe, we inherit the blessings to which baptism has entitled us.

But the receiving of the sign and seal, and the receiving of

---

[2] The Biblical Doctrine of Infant Baptism, page 72.
[3] Ecclesiastical Polity, V, lxiv, 4.
[4] *Institutes* IV.xvi.6.

16

the blessings signified, are not necessarily (or even normally) simultaneous. To *truly believing adults* the covenant sign of baptism (like circumcision to Abraham when he was ninety-nine years old) signifies and seals a grace which has already been received by faith. To *the infant seed* of believing parents, the covenant sign of baptism (like circumcision to Isaac at the age of eight days) is administered because they are born into the covenant and are thereby 'holy' in status (I Corinthians 7:14), but it signifies and seals to them graces which they still need to receive later by faith.

This is the case also with *adults* who are baptized *in unbelief* and later believe. We do not rebaptize them. Their baptism conveyed to them a title to the blessings of the New Covenant; they have now claimed their inheritance by faith. This point was established in the early centuries of the Church in the case of the *fictus,* the person baptized in a state of unworthiness. He was not rebaptized, because a distinction was drawn between the title or *character* of baptism, which was always conferred on the recipient, and the *grace* of baptism which depended on 'worthiness', i.e. repentance and faith.

This accepted view regarding unqualified adults the Reformers applied from adults to infants. Again, the baptism of infants

> has a suspended grace accompanying it, which comes into operation upon their growing up and becoming qualified for it.[5]

> Baptism, correctly administered, has thus one effect which is universal and invariable, whatever be the state or condition of the baptized person at the time, *viz* a title or pledge for the grace of the sacrament upon worthiness.[6]

The grace of the sacrament is not tied to the time of its

---

[5] J. B. Mozley, *A Review of the Baptismal Controversy* (1862), pages 48-49.
[6] Mozley, pages 40-41.

administration.[7]

It is in this sense that the Articles refer to baptism as not only a sign of grace but a means of grace; and not only a sign, but an effectual sign of grace (Article 25), 'by the which God doth work invisibly in us, and doth not only quicken, but also strengthen and confirm our faith in him'. Since a sacrament is a visible word, and it is the function of God's word to arouse faith (Romans 10:17), the sacraments stimulate our faith to lay hold of the blessings which they signify and to which they entitle us.

So the sacrament conveys the grace it signifies, not by a mechanical process but by conferring on us a title to it and by arousing within us the faith to embrace it.

> As baptism administered to those of years is not effectual unless they believe, so we can make no comfortable use of our baptism administered in our infancy until we believe... All the promises of grace were in my baptism estated upon me, and sealed up unto me, on God's part; but then I come to have the profit and benefit of them when I come to understand what grant God, in baptism, hath sealed unto me, and actually to lay hold on it by faith.

So wrote Archbishop Ussher in his book *Body of Divinity.*

Similarly Jerome:

> They that receive not baptism with perfect faith, receive the water, but the Holy Ghost they receive not.

But in neither sacrament is the gift tied to the time of the sacrament's administration. It is possible to receive the sign before the gift, as is usual in the case of infants, or to receive the sign after the gift, as is usual in the case of adults.

The question may be asked why, if baptism does not by itself confer the graces it signifies (but rather a title to them), the

---

[7] Mozley, page 49.

Bible and Prayer Book sometimes speak as if they did. I have already mentioned such phrases as 'baptized into Christ' (Romans 6:3), 'as many as were baptized into Christ did put on Christ' (Galatians 3:27), 'baptism saves us' (1 Peter 3:21), and 'this child is regenerate' (*Book of Common Prayer*).

The answer is really quite simple. It is that neither the Bible nor the Prayer Book envisages the baptism of an unbeliever; they assume that the recipient is a true believer. And since 'baptism and faith are but the outside and the inside of the same thing' (James Denney), the blessings of the New Covenant are ascribed to baptism which really belong to faith (Galatians 3:26, 28). Jesus had said 'he that believes and is baptized shall be saved', implying that faith would precede baptism. So a profession of faith after hearing the gospel always preceded baptism in Acts. For instance, 'they that received the word were baptized' (2:41), 'they believed Philip preaching... and were baptized' (8:12), 'Lydia gave heed to what was said by Paul. And when she was baptized...' (16:14,15), 'believe in the Lord Jesus Christ, and you will be saved...' (16:31-33).

It is the same in the Prayer Book service. There is no baptism in the Church of England except the baptism of a professing believer, adult or infant. The *adult* candidate's declaration of repentance, faith and surrender is followed by baptism and the declaration of regeneration. The same is true of an *infant* in the 1662 service, where it is not the godparents who speak for the child so much as the child who is represented as speaking through his sponsors. The child declares his or her repentance, faith and surrender, and desire for baptism. The child is then baptized and declared regenerate. So he is regenerate, in the same sense as he is a repentant believer in Jesus Christ, namely in the language of anticipatory faith or of sacraments.

It is in this sense too that we must understand the Catechism statement 'I was made a child of God'. It is sacramental language. I was 'made' a child of God in baptism, because baptism gave me a title to this privilege, not because baptism conferred this status on me irrespective of whether I believed or not.

J. B. Mozley writes of 'a class of statements which are literal in form, but hypothetical in meaning'. Again, he says it is 'a literal statement intended to be understood hypothetically'.[8]

## 3.     Conclusion

Does it matter whether we teach that the sign and the gift, the sacrament and the grace, are always received simultaneously, or generally separately?

Yes, it does matter. People need to be warned, for the good of their soul, that the reception of the sign, although it entitles them to the gift, does not confer the gift on them. They need to be taught the indispensable necessity of personal repentance and faith if they are to receive the thing signified. The importance of this may be seen in three spheres.

### 3.1.     The doctrine of assurance.

There is a great danger in post-Christian society of people trusting in baptism itself for salvation, and thus having a false sense of security. It is true that baptism is intended to bring us assurance, but how? Not by the mere fact of its administration, but because as a visible word of God it signifies his promises and evokes our faith in them. True assurance depends on a worthy reception of baptism.

### 3.2.     The discipline of baptism.

We are familiar with Bonhoeffer's castigation of the modem tendency to cheapen grace:

> The price we are having to pay today in the shape of the collapse of organized religion is only the inevitable

---

[8] Mozley, page 241.

consequence of our policy of making grace available at all too low a cost. We gave away the word and sacraments wholesale; we baptized, confirmed and absolved a whole nation without asking awkward questions, or insisting on strict conditions. Our humanitarian sentiment made us give that which was holy to the scornful and unbelieving. We poured forth unending streams of grace. But the call to follow Jesus was hardly ever heard. Where were those truths which impelled the early Church to institute the catechumenate, which enabled a strict watch to be kept over the frontier between the Church and the world, and afforded adequate protection for costly grace? ... To baptize infants without bringing them up in the life of the Church is not only an abuse of the sacrament, it betokens a disgusting frivolity in dealing with the souls of the children themselves. For baptism can never be repeated.[9]

And to quote from a sermon preached by the Rev H Hensley Henson[10] before the University of Oxford in 1896: 'The modern practice of unconditioned, indiscriminate baptizing is indecent in itself, discreditable to the Church and highly injurious to religion.'

Not that Scripture authorizes us to stand in judgment on the reality of people's profession. Professor John Murray's distinction is that God reserves the right to admit people to the *invisible* Church, on their *exercise* of faith. He delegates to ministers the responsibility to admit to the *visible* church, on their *profession* of faith.

Some would say that it must be a *credible* profession, but then we begin to make arbitrary rules by which to assess credibility. Our task is to be faithful in teaching the *significance* of baptism and the *conditions* of its efficacy; and then not to baptize any but those who profess to be penitent believers, and their children.

---

[9] D. Bonhoeffer, *The Cost of Discipleship* (1957), pages 47 and 179.
[10] Bishop of Durham (1920-39).

## 3.3. *The practice of evangelism.*

The baptized may still need to be evangelized, that is, exhorted to repentance, faith, and surrender so as to enter into the blessings pledged to them in baptism. But if all the baptized are regenerate, we cannot evangelize them. We can treat them as backsliders and urge them to return, but we cannot summon them to come to Christ if they are already in Christ by baptism. Thus the *ex opere operato* view cuts the nerve of evangelism, and we are back where Whitefield found himself on his return from Georgia in 1738. He was eyed with suspicion by the bulk of the clergy as a fanatic. According to Bishop Ryle, 'They were especially scandalized by his preaching the doctrine of regeneration or the new birth, as a thing which many baptized persons greatly needed'!

**Editor's note:** This article was first published in *The Anglican Synthesis – Essays by Catholics and Evangelicals* in 1964 and also appeared in *Churchman* 112/1 (1998).

# Baptism in the Book of Common Prayer

BY J. ALEC MOTYER

1.  The Unity of Baptism and the Lord's Supper in One Identical Sacramental Principle............................ 26
1.1.  Scripture Teaching................................................27
1.2.  Baptism..............................................................27
1.3.  Covenant Ordinances..............................................29
1.4.  The Covenant ......................................................29
1.5.  The Covenant and the Anglican Formularies.................31

2.  The Association between Regeneration and Baptism .... 33
2.1.  Regeneration in Scripture........................................34
2.2.  Scriptural statements on baptism...............................35
2.3.  Sacramental Efficacy..............................................36
2.4.  The Sacraments and Obedience..................................40
2.5.  An Instrument .....................................................41

3.  The Identity of Meaning between Adult and Infant Baptism ................................................................42
3.1.  The Ground of Baptism............................................43
3.2.  Adults...............................................................44
3.3.  Infants..............................................................44
3.4.  Faith and Baptism.................................................49
3.5.  Faith confessed....................................................50
3.6.  Appropriating faith ..............................................50
3.7.  The state of the baptized........................................50

# Baptism in the Book of Common Prayer

There are three places in the Book of Common Prayer which provide evidence concerning the baptismal teaching of the Church of England. In any discussion of the doctrine of our Church, pride of place, in every sense, must be given to the Thirty-nine Articles. Article 25 deals with the Sacraments, and Article 27 deals specifically with Baptism, and together they furnish the precise theological formulation of the doctrine. Secondly, there is the Catechism, and, thirdly, the two baptismal services.

*(i)      The Nature of the Evidence*
It is useful to remind ourselves at the outset that there is a distinction in the nature of the evidence provided by these three sources. The Articles furnish succinct and accurately worded theological statements, which are to be understood in their plain, straightforward, grammatical sense.[1] But the Catechism and the Services fall into a different category of evidence, and care must be taken to observe this difference when drawing deductions from them. In the Catechism and the Services of the Prayer Book, baptismal doctrine is applied to 'ideal' cases. It would be wrong, for example, to conclude in a superficial way that, because the Service includes the words, 'seeing now that this child is regenerate', therefore the Church of England teaches automatic and invariable regeneration in baptism. Evidence improperly used ceases to be valid evidence on the point.

In the Catechism and Services, the doctrine is brought into

---

[1] Cf. His Majesty's Declaration, prefixed to the Articles: "And that no man hereafter shall either print, or preach, to draw the Article aside any way, but shall submit to it in the plain and full meaning thereof: and shall not put his own sense or comment to be the meaning of the Article, but shall take it in the literal and grammatical sense."

relation to cases supposed to be in every way ideal, and we must interpret the evidence in that light. The distinction may be drawn as follows: the words of the Articles are to be taken as they stand, and in the meaning they clearly possess; they are true always, in all circumstances, without qualification or condition. But, because a human and personal factor is involved in the Catechism and the Services – in the one case the pupil, and in the other the candidate – individual cases can only be *presumptively* true, depending on whether the pupil and candidate are all they ought, in the circumstances, to be.[2]

## (ii)    The Scope of the Paper

For the purposes of this paper, some concise limitation of the subject must be adopted. There are three topics which may be said to arise out of any attentive reading of the Articles, the Catechism, and the Services: Firstly, there is the unity of Baptism and the Lord's Supper in one identical sacramental principle. Briefly, to illustrate this point, it is wrong to pin any meaning on the one sacrament which, other things being equal, would involve a wrong sacramental meaning when applied to the other. That such a unity of sacramental principle is taught by the Church of England is plainly implied in the fact that an Article on sacraments as such precedes the Articles dealing separately with the two dominical sacraments. It will be the first purpose of this study to attempt to discover and state that principle.

Secondly, an association between baptism and regeneration is taught with emphasis. This lies on the surface of all the documents, being particularly clear in the Services. But what is the nature of the association, and how are we to define it? Under this

---

[2] See J. B. Mozley, *The Baptismal Controversy,* pages 253ff for a full and reasoned exposition of this important point. "A catechism is a kind of formulary which admits of presumptive statements, i.e., that are literal in form but hypothetical in meaning... The child, being introduced, is presumed to be in the spiritual condition in which a Christian child ought to be, and to have the wishes, aims, and resolutions proper to his calling... They are obviously put into the child's mouth on the presumptive principle."

heading we will be led to discuss the efficacy of the sacrament, and its relation to the blessings associated with it.

The third point arising from our documents is the identity of meaning of adult and infant baptism. There is some current vogue for the suggestion that adult baptism is the norm, and that some fundamental modification is necessary in order to admit the baptism of infants at all. Some would even wish to see the Prayer Book printed differently, so that the service for adults came first, as though to present the candidature of infants first were to begin with something peculiar, something involving adjustment, or modification, if not actually misrepresentation of the real thing – as if, for example, a book on the science of optics should begin by saying what happens when the eyeball is squeezed between the fingers![3] But this is not the position which our documents adopt. They profess an identity of meaning while providing for a diversity of candidates. The importance of this for baptismal theology cannot be overstressed, as will become plain when we reach that concluding section of the paper.

1. *The Unity of Baptism and the Lord's Supper in One Identical Sacramental Principle*

It has already been observed that the Articles find it necessary to define the idea of sacraments as such (Article 25) before they embark upon the theological exposition of the individual sacraments (Articles 27 - 28). This is tantamount to saying that underlying the diversity of the two sacraments ordained by Christ our Lord there is a single basic principle, the sacramental principle, in the light of which each sacrament, separately considered, is to be understood. The last paragraph of Article 25 is specially noteworthy in this connection. 'The Sacraments,' it teaches, 'were not ordained

---

[3] Cf. the report, *Baptism and Confirmation,* page x: "In the New Testament Adult Baptism is the norm, and it is only in the light of this fact that the doctrine and practice of Baptism can be understood... The Baptism and Confirmation of Adults is treated as the archetypal service, and is printed first."

of Christ to be gazed upon, or to be carried about, but that we should duly use them.' No one, however, seems at any time to have thought of using baptism as a thing to be thus abused! But our reformers were so aware of an identity of sacramental principle that they instanced an error which had only been applied to the Holy Communion, and insisted that it would be an equal misuse of the other sacrament.

## 1.1.    Scripture Teaching

There is, then, according to our Church, one sacramental principle. Since the Articles willingly submit themselves to the touchstone of Holy Scripture, it is only proper that at this point we should turn to the Bible in an attempt to discover whether it also teaches such a single principle underlying the gospel sacraments, and what that principle is.

## 1.2.    Baptism

In connection with baptism, there are three relevant passages of Scripture:

(1) 1 Peter 3:20-22: 'they formerly did not obey, when God's patience waited in the days of Noah, while the ark was being prepared, in which a few, that is, eight persons, were brought safely through water. Baptism, which corresponds to this, now saves you, not as a removal of dirt from the body but as an appeal to God for a good conscience, through the resurrection of Jesus Christ.' It is well known in how many ways this passage is a crux of interpretation. But this much is unmistakable, lying on the very surface of the verses: Peter says that baptism is to be understood by means of an analogy with God's dealings with Noah, and specifically with the water of the flood, and the provision of the ark as a means of salvation.

(2) 1 Corinthians 10:1-13: 'I want you to know, brothers, that our fathers were all under the cloud, and all passed through the sea, and all were baptized into Moses in the cloud and in the sea.'

These opening verses must for the moment suffice to furnish the general drift and point of the passage. Paul, speaking of those early events in the history of the people of God, can refer to them as 'baptism'. He does not qualify the idea at all. He says directly: 'they were baptized'. Here again, then, we may with confidence find valid teaching about the Christian sacrament. And, for the present, it is enough to note that baptism is related to the dealings of God with Israel at the time of the Exodus.

(3) Colossians 2:11-12: 'In him also [that is, in Christ] you were circumcised with a circumcision made without hands, by putting off the body of the flesh, by the circumcision of Christ, having been buried with him in baptism.' Fuller treatment of this verse must be reserved for a later stage in the discussion. At present, let it suffice to point out that baptism is described as 'the circumcision of Christ', and that this fact alone – however it must ultimately be understood – brings the Christian ordinance into direct contact with God's ancient dealings with Abraham.[4]

---

[4] Needless to say the assertion of a parallel between baptism and circumcision is a crux in the baptismal controversy, and those holding the 'Baptist' position resist the aligning of the two covenant signs. This position may be found simply stated in H. H. Rowley: *The Unity of the Bible,* chapter VI. However, the evidence – additional to the detailed treatment of Colossians 2:10-13 which follows later in the present essay – is considerable for adopting the view that the signs are continuous with each other within their own covenants. It would be very hard, for example, to say in quite what way God fulfilled his promise that the covenant of circumcision with Abraham would be 'everlasting' (Genesis 17:13), if, in fact, it altogether drops from the Church of God at the time of Christ and finds no continuance whatsoever. This would be a peculiar type of everlasting-ness. Or again, apart from the close parallel between circumcision and baptism it is hard to see how Paul can say of Christians: 'We are the circumcision' (Philippians 3:3). There is also the evidence of the idea of a 'seal'. In Romans 4:11 circumcision is called a seal, and in 2 Corinthians 1:21-22, and Ephesians 1:13 the same word probably refers to baptism, an interpretation based on the use of the word 'anointed' in 2 Corinthians 1:21 (cf. Acts 10:38, referring to the baptism of Jesus), and on the order of words 'heard ... believed ... sealed' in Ephesians 1:13 (cf. Acts 18:8: 'hearing, believed, and were baptized'). The metaphor of the seal is implicit in the notion of baptism as 'burial', for burial is the final seal on a duly certified death.

## 1.3.  *Covenant Ordinances*

These three passages all really speak to the same point. They take up the three great covenant situations of the Old Testament – Noah, Abraham, and Moses – and teach that it is in the light of them that baptism is to be understood. Exactly the same position is reached by considering scriptures relative to the Lord's Supper.

(1). In Matthew 26:27-28 we have the words of our Lord Jesus Christ concerning the supper which he instituted: 'And he took a cup, and when he had given thanks he gave it to them, saying, "Drink of it, all of you, for this is my blood of the covenant."' Our Lord was re-echoing and, in a sense, recapitulating the words of Moses to Israel on Mount Sinai: 'Behold, the blood of the covenant' (Exodus 24:8).

(2). Paul (1 Corinthians 11:25) speaks to the same point: 'In the same way also he took the cup, after supper, saying, "This cup is the new covenant in my blood."' Paul conflates here two Old Testament passages. The association of 'covenant' and 'blood' is unmistakably a 'Passover' reference, so that the apostle, like his Lord, is linking himself directly to Moses. But the wording, 'new covenant', recalls the prophecy of Jeremiah (31:31) that God will enter upon a new undertaking with his people, based (v. 34) on a final and complete dealing with their sin.

Thus the two gospel sacraments have a common root in Scripture in the covenant idea.


## 1.4.  *The Covenant*

Two remarks concerning the covenant may be made here. Firstly, the covenant is a movement of grace from God to man. This is particularly noticeable in the covenant which God made with Noah. The first fact which the Scripture teaches about Noah is that he 'found grace in the eyes of the Lord' (Genesis 6:8).[5] The verb

---

[5] It is very noticeable how Genesis separates off 6:9 from 6:8 by making a new

'found' must not be understood to imply that Noah in any way merited God's favour – the very idea of 'grace' excludes the possibility of 'merit'. In fact, the real meaning of the words, 'Noah found grace', would be better expressed by saying that grace found Noah! The Lord, acting in sovereign initiative, made his hand to rest upon the man he had chosen. This is the characteristic 'covenant situation': in a day of worldwide judgment, God wills to save a people for himself. Apart from the covenant they would share the judgment which on every personal ground, they, with all mankind, deserved; and apart from the gracious initiative of God in marking them off for himself, they would not be brought into the divine covenant.

Secondly, this fundamental covenant idea – the movement of God towards man in grace – finds expression in the covenant signs, and most notably in the sign of circumcision. It is very important to observe how the verses and the teaching flow along in Genesis 17. In verse 4, God begins to declare his covenant in a series of divine promises. These involve three distinct things – on the human side, a numerous and distinguished posterity (vv. 4-6); on the spiritual side, a spiritual relationship to God for Abraham and his descendants for ever (v. 7); and, on the territorial side, the inheritance of the promised land (v. 8).

Following upon this definition of the covenant as a series of divine promises to Abraham and his descendants, the covenant is, secondly, defined as a sign which Abraham is to wear on his body (v. 10): 'This is my covenant... every male among you shall be circumcised.' The sign must express what that covenant is – namely, a manward movement of the grace of God. Consequently the covenant sign is God's mark upon the covenant man. It is not, in its proper meaning, the covenant-man's response to God. It is God's marking of a chosen man, and saying of him that he is a

---

beginning. Thus we are forbidden to understand that it was the superior moral character of Noah which led to his being chosen by God. Rather we must interpret 6:8 as giving us the secret history of Noah, and 6:9 as describing the *consequent* public life.

man of the covenant. The very fact that Abraham made the covenant sign upon himself and his family necessarily involved his response to God. But that response is not the idea of the sign as such. The covenant came to Abraham verbally and visibly: verbally it is the declaration of the promises; visibly it is the sign which God ordained as a mark upon the recipient of the promises.

## 1.5.    *The Covenant and the Anglican Formularies*

With these thoughts in mind, we can say that in the *Book of Common Prayer* baptism is set before us as a covenant ordinance. The word 'covenant' is not used in any of the four baptismal sections of the Prayer Book, but the features of God's covenant dealing are very present and very evident.[6] Article 25 begins to make this basic conception plain. The sacraments are 'certain sure witnesses, and effectual signs of grace, and God's good will towards us'. That is to say, the sacraments express a movement of grace which begins in God and reaches out to man. These sacraments are 'ordained of Christ our Lord in the Gospel's, just as the covenant signs in the Old Testament had God as their Author.

Article 27 teaches that in baptism the promises of God, 'the promises of forgiveness of sin, and of our adoption to be the sons of God by the Holy Ghost, are visibly signed and sealed'. Baptism seals the promises – which is exactly the function performed towards Abraham by circumcision.

Amongst these promises is that of our sonship by adoption. Sonship was the central feature of God's redemptive programme in Egypt: 'Israel is my firstborn son' (Exodus 4:22). Once again, therefore, an implicitly covenantal idea is advanced by our formularies. Finally, in Article 27, though it anticipates a

---

[6] The absence of the explicit use of the word 'covenant' is, of course, greatly to be regretted. The framers of the service proposed in the report *Baptism and Confirmation* have only healed this wound slightly by including Hebrews 13:20-21. This merely verbal introduction of the word 'covenant' is small compensation if one had to exchange the old service for the new.

discussion yet to come, the reference to the baptism of young children is the clearest indication that the Church of England thinks of baptism as a covenant ordinance, because the justification of infant baptism is this, that it is demanded by God's covenant dealing. The God of the covenant of grace always addresses himself 'to you and to your offspring after you' (Genesis 17:7).

In the baptismal services the same note is continued. The first actual prayer in the service reminds us of Noah and his family in the ark, and of the people of Israel led safely through the Red Sea, so that, from the outset, a covenant setting is achieved for the administration of the sacrament. Equally, the vows which are made in the service, to renounce, believe, and keep, are again part of the covenant arrangement. Genesis 17 displays the two sides of the covenant, which later were to receive such prominent and full elaboration through the mediation of Moses. On God's side there is the 'I make' (17:2); and on man's side there is the 'you keep' (17:9). The same grace which makes the covenant exacts a response from the recipient, a grateful response of sole-loyalty and sole-obedience to the Covenant-Maker. Abram was commanded: 'walk before me, and be blameless' (Genesis 17:1); Moses 'came and told the people all the words of the LORD and all the rules. And all the people answered with one voice and said, "All the words that the LORD has spoken we will do."' (Exodus 24:3). The covenant involves the idea of responsive dedication, such that the greatest act of grace the Old Testament knows, 'I am the LORD your God, who brought you out of the land of Egypt,' is necessarily followed by the greatest moral demand which the world has ever heard, 'You shall have no other gods before me.' Thus the very idea of baptismal vows enforces the covenant orientation of the service.

A third feature of the service may be noted as evidence for the same truth: the very heart of the service: baptism 'into the name of the Father, and of the Son, and of the Holy Ghost'. The declaration of the name of God was the climax of the divine revelation to Israel at the time of the Exodus (3:13ff.; 6:1ff.), so that

Israel became henceforth the people upon whom the name of God was called.[7] When God brought people near to himself, it is as though he marked the intimacy thus established by allowing the privileged ones to know him by a special title or name which summarized his self-revelation to them. To Abram, he came as *El Shaddai* (Genesis 17:1), the God who confronts man when all hope is spent, and brings his miraculous, transforming promises to pass.[8] To Israel in Egypt, God revealed the meaning of his personal name, *Yahweh*, the God who redeems his people and overthrows his enemies. To the Christian, at the moment of the sealing of the New Covenant to him, the final revelation is expressed: the name in all its fullness, the supreme privilege, the knowledge of the Father and the Son and the Holy Ghost, the Trinity himself, God perfectly made known.

In baptism, therefore, we are dealing with a covenant ordinance, a movement of grace which reaches out from God to men; and when we speak of the baptismal sign we mean the donation by God, through his ministers, of the mark of the New Covenant.

## 2.    *The Association between Regeneration and Baptism*

Whether we consider the high moments of baptismal controversy – Gorham and the Bishop of Exeter – or the personal difficulties of many an ordinary Anglican concerning baptism, this is the crux of the problem. The formularies insist on bringing baptism and regeneration together. How is the relationship to be accurately defined and understood?

Article 27 says explicitly that 'baptism is also a sign of regeneration or new birth'. At the baptismal services (and both services are alike in this respect, as in most others), after the

---

[7] E.g., Jeremiah 14:9, etc.
[8] The actual meaning of *El Shaddai* as a description of God is in some doubt. The use of the title in Genesis fully bears out the description of the divine nature indicated. See J. A. Motyer, *The Revelation of the Divine Name* (Tyndale Press).

baptism of the candidate in the name of the Trinity, the minister declares: 'Seeing now dearly beloved brethren, that these persons/this child are/is regenerate.' And, finally, in the Catechism, the child, when asked from whom he received his name, replies: 'My Godfathers and my Godmothers in my baptism; wherein I was made a member of Christ, the child of God, and an inheritor of the kingdom of heaven.' Thus, at every point, regeneration is declared to be the particular grace of baptism. This is the association we must now try to understand.

## 2.1.    *Regeneration in Scripture*

Our first move, once more, will be to take the matter to Holy Scripture, and to discern some of the things it says about regeneration. There is, in fact, quite a wide vocabulary of regeneration in the New Testament. It is spoken of under many figures. Firstly, and chiefly, there is the figure of new birth, as expressed by our Lord in John 3:3, 'unless one is born again he cannot see the kingdom of God.' There is, secondly, the related figure of Sonship – in John 1:12-13, 'to all who did receive him, who believed in his name, he gave the right to become children of God, who were born, not of blood nor of the will of the flesh nor of the will of man, but of God.' The regenerate is a person who has been 'born of God' and is a son of God. The third figure used concerning this marvellous work of God in imparting new life is the figure of resurrection, or of being quickened with Christ. Ephesians 2:1 reveals the condition of the sinner by nature: 'you were dead in [your] trespasses and sins.' But verse 4 marks a great change, declaring how God has acted in this situation: 'But God, being rich in mercy, because of the great love with which he loved us, even when we were dead in our trespasses, made us alive together with Christ.' That which is dead, by very definition, contains no life, and contains no possibility of itself producing life. Into this situation of hopelessness, immobility, and helplessness, God has come with life-giving purpose.

## 2.2.   *Scriptural statements on baptism*

These three figures of regeneration – being born again, born of
God, and raised from the dead – are particularly important for our
study, because, in the New Testament, in connection with each of
them, there is a statement concerning baptism which is pretty well
identical with the words quoted above from the *Book of Common
Prayer.*

(1) John 3:5 is well understood as a reference to baptism.[9]
Our Lord says: 'unless one is born of water and the Spirit, he
cannot enter the kingdom of God.' Some urge that this is a
reference to natural birth followed by spiritual birth, and no more;
and that our Lord was here teaching the need for the 'second birth'
through the agency of the Holy Spirit. True as this is in itself, there
does not seem to be any warrant in Scripture for making 'water' a
symbol of natural birth. In context, the passage proceeds to refer to
John's baptism, and the controversy about purification. This would
suggest that our Lord is here offering an anticipatory word about
the full ordinance of Christian baptism. John baptized with water,
and, at the same time, prophesied of one 'who will baptize you with
the Holy Spirit'. Jesus links the two ideas together (as they were
linked in his own baptism) by saying, 'unless one is born of water
and the Spirit....' This, then, would be a statement about baptism of
the same calibre as the words of the Prayer Book that 'these
persons are regenerate'. Both have the same unequivocal air of
stating a fact, as they link together the outward element and the
spiritual agency of God.

(2) Galatians 3:26-27 bring together baptism and sonship.

---

[9] Cf. William Hendriksen's comment *(The Gospel of John,* Banner of Truth Trust):
'The key to the interpretation of these words (i.e., John 3:5) is found in 1:22 (see
also 1:26, 31; cf. Matthew 3:11; Mark 1:8; Luke 3:16) where *water* and *Spirit* are
also found side by side in connection with baptism.' Hendriksen rightly goes on
to point out that the full force of the Lord's words is to teach that an outward
sign by itself is of no avail; it must have the spiritual reality of the power of the
Holy Spirit. This belongs to a later stage of our argument and may be left for the
moment.

Verse 26 reads: 'in Christ Jesus you are all sons of God, through faith'; and verse 27, with its initial word 'for' follows as an explanation of this fact of sonship by faith: 'For as many of you as were baptized into Christ have put on Christ.' Here, again, is a very radical statement about baptism, parallel to what the Prayer Book says, and amply justifying its language.[10]

(3) Turning finally to the figure of resurrection, the key passage is Romans 6:3-4. This is the strongest word Scripture has to say about baptism, and undoubtedly those who stumble at the wording of the *Book of Common Prayer* should long since have stumbled at the words of the apostle. It reads: 'Do you not know that all of us who have been baptized into Christ Jesus were baptized into his death? We were buried therefore with him by baptism into death, in order that, just as Christ was raised from the dead by the glory of the Father, we too might walk in newness of life.' In a completely unqualified manner, the apostle relates the possession and enjoyment of the benefits of the death and resurrection of Christ to the fact of baptism. Here is complete justification for the statement in the Prayer Book concerning Baptism and Regeneration. To observe that this is so is no small advance towards understanding the Anglican doctrine of baptism. At the very point where even some Anglicans themselves have uneasy consciences, the *Book of Common Prayer* is merely echoing the words and formulations of Holy Scripture.

## 2.3. *Sacramental Efficacy*

But we must go further than that, and ask what Scripture means when it makes such positive assertions about baptism. For it is

---

[10] Some may object here that Galatians 3:26-27 lack the full categorical force of the Prayer Book statement that 'these persons are regenerate' because of the occurrence of the words 'by faith' which introduce a qualifying idea. This is true enough, but, as will be shown later, the Prayer Book also insists on such qualifications. The Baptism Service includes the telling but (in controversy) often forgotten question: 'Wilt thou be baptized in this faith?' with the reply: 'That is my desire.' A later stage in our argument takes cognisance of these facts.

only when we arrive at a grasp of scriptural meaning that we will see how truly biblical is our Anglican formula.

There are two passages of Scripture which deal with the question of the efficacy of outward ordinances: Romans 2:25-29 and 1 Corinthians 10:1-13. Romans 2 is the central New Testament passage on the subject, and enunciates three basic principles:

### 2.3.1. *The outward sign conveys no benefit inevitably attached to it.*

Verse 28: 'no one is a Jew who is merely one outwardly.' A man may be circumcised according to the exactitude of the ritual and by a fully authorized priest, and yet not be a Jew. The outward sign conveys no benefit inevitably attached to it. But this is also part of what the New Testament teaches concerning baptism, as the story of Simon, in Acts 8, makes unmistakably clear. This is the only really fully-documented account of baptism which the New Testament contains, and it tells of a baptism which conveyed no spiritual benefit to the candidate.

Apparently the practice of the New Testament Church with adults coming into it from paganism was to require some intelligible profession of faith in Jesus Christ. Thus, 'Simon himself believed' (v. 13) and was baptized. But subsequently, through the joint evidence of life and doctrine, Peter (v. 21) does not hesitate to condemn him as having 'neither part nor lot in this matter, for your heart is not right before God'. Apparently his baptism had conveyed no benefit; it had not brought regeneration to Simon; he was still in the gall of bitterness and the bond of iniquity. The New Testament, therefore, shows concerning baptism what Paul urges concerning circumcision: that the outward ordinance conveys no benefit inevitably attached to it.

## 2.3.2. The outward ordinance conveys no benefit which cannot be had without it.

Verse 26: 'if a man who is uncircumcised keeps the precepts of the law, will not his uncircumcision be regarded as circumcision?' The Gentile never had the outward sign, but apparently he could have the status. His uncircumcision, the very fact that he never had the sign, could, in given circumstances, be reckoned as circumcision. The outward ordinance, then, conveys no benefit which may not be had without it.

But this also is taught in the New Testament concerning baptism. In Acts 2:38, Peter exhorts, 'Repent and be baptized every one of you in the name of Jesus Christ for the forgiveness of your sins, and you will receive the gift of the Holy Spirit.' Two great blessings are here associated with the ordinance of baptism: the remission of sins, and the gift of the Holy Spirit. But the New Testament also promises these without any reference to baptism at all. In Acts 13:38, we read: 'Let it be known to you therefore, brothers, that through this man forgiveness of sins is proclaimed to you, and by him everyone who believes is freed from everything.' There is no reference to any outward ordinance, but the gift is promised to those who place their trust in Jesus. In the same way, concerning the gift of the Holy Ghost, John 7:38-39 declares: 'Whoever believes in me, as the Scripture has said, "Out of his heart will flow rivers of living water." Now this he said about the Spirit, whom those who believed in him were to receive.' Again, there is no reference to baptism. And this is true throughout the whole of the New Testament. The benefits of Christ's redemption are offered without reference to outward signs, and it may be taken as a biblical principle that the ordinance can convey no benefit which cannot be had without it.[11]

---

[11] The Dying Thief is, of course, a classical example of divinely pledged salvation to one who never knew any sacramental rite. It is useless to urge that this is special pleading based on an exceptional case. The New Testament, as a whole, entirely

### 2.3.3. The enjoyment of the spiritual reality which God has associated with the outward ordinance depends on the relation of the heart towards God.

Verse 29: 'But a Jew is one inwardly, and circumcision is a matter of the heart, by the Spirit, not by the letter.' This principle is in accordance with everything which the Old Testament insists on concerning outward observance. It lies at the basis of the prophetic rebuke of mere ceremonialism. The God of the Bible is one who has ever appointed outward ordinances for the assistance and blessing of his people, but who has never found ultimate value in the mere performance of any rite. At Mount Sinai, it was the heart of the people which God desired, as he cried to Moses, 'Oh that they had such a mind as this always, to fear me and to keep all my commandments!' (Deuteronomy 5:29).

It was in the same spirit that he promised that when he re-gathered his people finally, then he himself would 'circumcise your heart and the heart of your offspring, so that you will love the LORD your God with all your heart' (Deuteronomy 30:6). Turning to the New Testament, we find this very same teaching on the point of baptism. In Acts 8:21-22, when Simon is found to be without any of the spiritual blessings which are associated with baptism, Peter lays the whole burden of explanation on the state of the man's heart towards God: 'your heart is not right before God. Repent, therefore, of this wickedness of yours, and pray to the Lord that, if possible, the intent of your heart may be forgiven you.' There is no power in the ordinance as such to effect its object. The power is that of God (cf. Colossians 2:13). Therefore Peter directs Simon to pray to God, the Author of the sacrament and the Bestower of its blessings. But the efficacy of the sacrament is known only where

---

lacks evidence to support the modern, so-called 'high' view of the sacraments. The very paucity of references to either of the sacraments – for example, there is no reference at all to the Lord's Supper in the Pastoral Epistles – ought to warn the modern church that it is out of step with the apostolic norm.

there is a heart right with God, and no outward correctness, whether of Orders of Ministry or exactitude of cultic performance, can replace this fundamentally necessary thing.

## 2.4.    *The Sacraments and Obedience*

We turn now to the second New Testament passage bearing on the efficacy of outward ordinances, 1 Corinthians 10:1-13. In these verses, Paul teaches that there were some people who had valid sacraments but never reached the land of Canaan. Such is the substance of his remarks in these thirteen verses. He says: 'I want you to know, brothers, that our fathers were all under the cloud, and all passed through the sea, and all were baptized into Moses in the cloud and in the sea, and all ate the same spiritual food, and all drank the same spiritual drink.'[12] So far Paul has taken care to draw a clear parallel between the fathers with their possession of certain outward signs and experiences, and his Corinthian readers with their possession of the Christian sacraments. He continues: 'Nevertheless, with most of them God was not pleased.' Apparently, participation in the sacraments brought no inevitable eternal security in attendance upon it. The displeasure of God was revealed in the wilderness overthrow.

This was not intended to be a matter of mere antiquarian interest to the Corinthians (or to us) for 'these things took place as examples for us' (verse 6), and 'were written down for our instruction, on whom the end of the ages has come. Therefore let anyone who thinks that he stands take heed lest he fall.' (verses 11-12). Paul was moved by an entirely practical concern for the church. Trust can be falsely placed as well as securely placed; the feet can be on sand as well as on rock. There is no security in outward

---

[12] This paper takes no notice at all of differences of opinion concerning the actual mode of baptism. Those who *insist* on total immersion ought, however, to find great difficulty with these verses in 1 Corinthians 10 which say that the Israelites were baptized in a cloud, that is, without water at all, and in the sea, where the whole essence of the miracle was that water never touched them. The same was true, of course, of Noah in the ark.

ordinances – not even dominical sacraments. Outward ordinances do not avail for people whose subsequent lives are disobedient to God.

Here were people who passed under the cloud, marking their separation to be God's people: to go where he went, to stay where he stayed; here were people who passed through the sea, marking their separation from the world, for the waters rolled back and cut off the Egyptians, and they saw the Egyptians dead on the shore. But when they went on, they did not go on with God, and they did not go on in separation. The outward signs proclaimed one thing to them, but found no response in their hearts, and no reflection in their lives. They were put on probation by the outward signs; they failed on probation, and they never reached the promised land. The promises were made, and sealed to them, but they never 'by faith and patience' (Hebrews 6:12) inherited the promises.

Likewise, the New Testament teaches concerning baptism. We noted that Peter (Acts 2:38-39) associated the gift of the Spirit with baptism, but Acts 5:32 speaks with another voice concerning 'the Holy Spirit, whom God has given to those who obey him'. The outward ordinance looks forward to the moral and spiritual consecration of the obedient life, apart from which it is a mere ceremony.

## 2.5.   *An Instrument*

Turning from the Bible to the *Book of Common Prayer*, we discover exactly the same teaching on the question of the efficacy of the rite. Article 27 links baptism with the spiritual blessings which have been promised in Scripture. It is a sign of regeneration, of the forgiveness of sins, and of our adoption to be the sons of God by the Holy Spirit. But there is the same insistence, as in Scripture, that these blessings are attached to baptism conditionally: not inevitably, but conditionally.

The mode in which baptism works is expressed in the

words: 'whereby, as by an instrument'. Putting the matter popularly, but none the less exactly, there are two sorts of instrument. There is the 'blunt instrument' which carries its effect inevitably with it. But there is also the 'legal instrument', which conveys its benefits only to the person who falls within its terms, thus acting not inevitably, but conditionally; not mechanically, but morally. The Prayer Book will admit the instrumentality of the sacraments only in the second sense. This same Article insists that baptism is effective in such as receive it 'rightly',[13] that is, with the correct inward disposition. The Catechism requires of persons to be baptized repentance and faith. The Services declare that 'after this promise made by Christ, you must faithfully and for your part promise'. There must be a responsive faith toward God before the promises are inherited.

The Prayer Book also concurs with Scripture in asserting that the power belongs to God and not to the sign. Article 27 emphasizes that faith is confirmed and grace increased by virtue of prayer unto God. The second prayer in the Service rests the efficacy of the ordinance upon the power of prayer: 'So give now unto us that ask.' In summary, then, the *Book of Common Prayer* says what Scripture says. It uses the same straightforward, radical, striking language as Scripture does, in associating the blessings with baptism; and then, like Scripture, it proceeds to insist that the outward signs are conditionally efficacious, being moral instruments of spiritual benefit.

### 3. The Identity of Meaning between Adult and Infant Baptism

The *Book of Common Prayer* teaches that adult and infant baptism

---

[13] Latin, '*recte*', with correct disposition; not 'rite', with correct outward form. Each of Articles 25-29 ought to be studied in detail to see how emphatically they assert the Receptionist Doctrine of the Sacraments – the necessity of the correct disposition in the recipient, as opposed to those who make a valid sacrament depend on either Orders or Ceremonial.

are identical rites. Article 27 begins by speaking of baptism, without any reference to the age of the candidate. Its concluding sentence affirms that the baptism of young children is in anywise to be retained as conformable to the mind of Christ in the matter. There is no suggestion that the baptism mentioned in the last sentence is any different from that which is defined at the beginning. Rather the inference would be that the subject is the same throughout, and that, doctrinally, the age of the candidate is a matter of indifference.

Before noting the evidence of the Catechism on this point, it is useful to be reminded what this document is: 'An instruction to be learned of every person'. It does not only instruct the child, but also the adult who has been baptized. For all learners alike it proposes the same baptismal doctrine, and the only distinction it makes in the matter of baptizing infants is to answer a query that arises administratively: how can infants be baptized if they cannot profess repentance and faith? If the Catechism envisaged that infant baptism required some doctrinal adaption, it must say so at this place but, in fact, it does nothing of the kind. The problem is seen as administrative, and the office of god-parenthood is offered as the solution.

Of course, the chief evidence that the Church of England affirms the doctrinal identity of adult and infant baptism is to be found in the fact that it proposes identical services for each candidate, the alterations made being dictated by the occasion and not by any theological consideration.

## 3.1.   *The Ground of Baptism*

The identity of the doctrine of baptism in spite of the diversity of candidates may be further demonstrated by asking on what ground baptism rests. What is our warrant for baptizing? That both adult and infant baptism are susceptible of the same answer is the final proof that the baptism of infants is not in any sense a special adaption of sound doctrine. In a word, the answer is this: we baptize in every case because of a command of God to do so.

## 3.2.   *Adults*

For adults, we have the word of the Lord Jesus Christ: 'Whoever believes and is baptized will be saved' (Mark 16:16).[14] The commandment of the Lord is that believing adults shall be baptized. The case of Simon, unhappy though it is, shows us that this was indeed what the early church did, for (Acts 8:13) 'Simon himself believed' and was baptized. Apparently, he gave to the church some intelligible and satisfactory account of faith in Christ, and when they accepted his self-testimony and baptized him, they were following the command of the Lord Jesus himself. In the service for Adult Baptism, Mark 16:16 is one of the items peculiar to that service, showing our awareness that the baptism of the believing adult finds its ground in a command of the Lord.

## 3.3.   *Infants*

But we accept the same ground for infant baptism. There is no other warrant than that God has commanded that it shall be done. The evidence here is stronger: it rests not just on this verse and that, but on the demonstrable unity of the whole Scripture.

Baptism, as we saw, is a covenant ordinance. But the fundamental promise of the covenant, as expressed to Abraham, included his descendants: he promised to be 'God to you and to your offspring after you' (Genesis 17:7). Consequently, Abraham's first act of obedience to God under the covenant was to circumcise himself and his child. Thus God had commanded, and thus he did. For God had made it clear to Abraham that 'your offspring' was not to be taken to mean 'children after they have grown to years of discretion and have decided for themselves', but specifically was defined as the eight-day-old infant.[15] The sign marks the recipient

---

[14] Mark 16:16 shows clearly that spiritual potency is not to be looked for in the rite of baptism itself, even though it be a divine requirement. Condemnation arises entirely out of lack of faith, i.e. whether a person be baptized or not, if he does not believe, he is lost.

[15] It seems likely that, in Abraham's time, circumcision was practised widely in

of the covenant promises. God's promise embraces the parent and his child, and it is the obedience of the covenant parent to pass on and confer the sign to the child.

This basic covenant practice is carried over into the New Testament by certain well-known scriptures, of which we will examine four:

(1) Our Lord's teaching in Mark 10:13-16: The argument often levelled against this passage, that because baptism is not mentioned in it, therefore it can have nothing to do with baptism, is too superficial to warrant reply. John 6 contains no reference to the Lord's Supper, but has it, for that reason, nothing to teach us about a fruitful feeding upon Christ in the Supper?

There are two specially noteworthy features in this passage in Mark. Firstly, there is the Lord's assertion that children[16] are model members of the kingdom. He says that the kingdom belongs to them, and that everyone who would enter the kingdom must become like a little child. However, it was the Lord himself who associated baptism and kingdom-membership, when he said: 'unless one is born of water and the Spirit, he cannot enter the kingdom of God' (John 3:5).[17] There was no need whatsoever for the Lord to elaborate in this way upon his indignation at the disciples' rejection of the children. Why did he thus introduce the concept of kingdom-membership into the discussion, unless he wished to emphasize that under the New Covenant children occupy the same place as under the Old?

---

surrounding heathen nations, but, as a social rite, admitting to full tribal membership, it was a puberty rite, or a preliminary to marriage. It is significant, therefore, that when, for Abraham, it came to have an exclusively religious significance – membership of the Church – it was moved back to infancy.

[16] Mark uses the word *paidion,* used of an infant just born (John 16:21), and of a child recently born (Matthew 2:8). Luke (18:15) uses *brephos,* which could only mean here a new born child (cf. Luke 2:12, 16; 1 Peter 2:2, etc.).

[17] In our Lord's association of baptism and kingdom, it is noteworthy that his own baptism was followed by a contest based on possession of the kingdom. Note, also, the word *paliggenesia,* as used in Matthew 19:28 it refers to the kingdom of Christ fully come, whereas in Titus 3:5 it is associated with 'water and Spirit'.

In the second place, we must note the Lord's actions: 'he took them in his arms and blessed them, laying his hands on them.' His action was public, deliberate, and emphatic. He acted as one wishing to call attention to what he was doing; as one desiring to make an impression. He also acted as one who proposed to impart a blessing: 'he repeatedly and fervently blessed them' – the verb is intensive in formation, and describes repeated action.[18] Either the Lord Jesus was perpetrating a spiritual hoax for the sentimental satisfaction of doting mothers, or else he saw babies as proper recipients of divine blessing, and proceeded to bestow such a blessing upon them. This is so manifestly the point of view of the covenant of grace that we have no option but to hold that the Lord was here deliberately prolonging its operation into that final covenant of which he himself is the Founder and Federal Head.

(2) The teaching of Peter in Acts 2:39: 'For the promise is for you and for your children.' Peter, let it be remembered, was addressing an exclusively Jewish congregation. It is surely an intolerable gloss on his words, and one which his hearers would never have considered possible or intended, to make them mean 'your children, provided always that they have grown up and have decided for themselves'. Peter is virtually quoting the covenant promise of Genesis 17:7, and he is acting entirely in consonance with the principles of the covenant as God proposed them to Abraham. He is declaring that just as children were welcomed *de jure,* into the Old Covenant, so, also, they are welcomed into the new. And, furthermore, he spoke these words in a baptismal context. Why should he mention the children of the first converts at all, if he did not wish to assert their right to the same covenant sign which he was proposing for their parents?

(3) Colossians 2:10-13. The subject matter of these verses is the wholesale and miraculous transformation which takes place when a man becomes a Christian. Firstly, we note what is the state of man without Christ (v. 13). The natural man is dead. The verse

---

[18] *Kateulogei.*

offers a double explanation of this state of death: on the one hand, it has been brought about by 'trespasses'. Sin is a deadly destroyer, and the sinner is his own executioner. On the other hand, the state of death remains because God has made no move to implement a change: death is equated with 'uncircumcision'.

Secondly, this situation of death, with its twin causes, has been remedied by a double act of God. The deadly 'trespasses' have been cancelled in forgiveness, and all their death-dealing sting has been exhausted upon the crucified Christ (vv. 13b, 14); and the deadness of uncircumcision has been transformed into life by a quickening which God has accomplished.

Because of this, in the third place, the Christian who has been 'made full' in Christ (v. 10) is spoken of as 'circumcised' (v. 11). Whatever is the reality of which circumcision is the sign, the Christian possesses that reality. If we consider the actual circumcision of Abraham, particularly as Paul sees and understands it, there is a remarkable fulness and appropriateness of teaching. According to Genesis 17, circumcision marks the recipient of the covenant promises. In the case of Abraham, personally considered, the promise was of a transformation which can rightly be called regeneration: he became a new man; Abram was changed to Abraham; the man who was personally incapable of becoming the father of the promised seed is turned into a man capable of fathering a multitude of nations. In Romans 4:18ff, Paul says that Abraham was transformed from death to life, through the power of God, and the appropriating agency of faith. In the same way, the Christian is circumcised in Christ. It is a spiritual transaction, leaving no bodily mark, for it is 'not made with hands'; it signifies a total change of nature, 'the putting off of the body of the flesh'; it is 'the circumcision of Christ', the mark which Christ, the Head of the Church, sets upon the members of the New Covenant.

Fourthly, and finally, all this is related to and explained by

Christian baptism. According to the construction of the sentence,[19] the relation of the main verb, 'you were circumcised', to the participle, 'having been buried', is either: 'You were baptized, and so are circumcised' – baptism being the antecedent action, or 'At baptism you were circumcised' – the two being simultaneous. Thus baptism and circumcision are equated, each within its own covenant.[20] But the equation does not depend solely upon a feature of syntax; it is also necessitated by similarity of teaching. Before baptism the person is dead, for baptism is a *burial,* not an execution. In baptism, there is a resurrection in Christ, through the power of God, and the appropriating agency of faith. Thus, the whole passage is integrated around the death-resurrection motif, and the substance is stated twice over: firstly, in relation to the transition from uncircumcision to circumcision, and secondly, in the transition from unbaptism to baptism. In the most emphatic possible way, Paul unifies the covenant mercies of God. It is peculiarly relevant to our present purpose to note that he expresses no qualification whatever. As circumcision operated; so baptism operates.

(4) The final Scripture to be considered, as we seek to show how the New Testament carries over the covenant theology of the Old Testament, is 1 Corinthians 7:14: 'Otherwise your children

---

[19] A. T. Robertson: *A Grammar of the Greek New Testament in the light of Historical Research,* page 860. The aorist participle expresses *'Antecedent Action.* This is the usual idiom with the circumstantial participle. This is the most common use of the Aorist participle. But it must not be forgotten that the aorist participle does not in itself mean antecedent action.... That is suggested by the context.' Cf. Mark 1:31; Colossians 1:3-4; etc. 'But *Simultaneous Action* is common also.... Here, again it is a matter of suggestion.... Indeed, this simultaneous action is in exact harmony with the punctiliar meaning of the aorist tense.' Cf. Mark 15:30; Acts 15:8. '... *Subsequent Action* is not expressed by the Aorist Participle.' C. F. D. Moule, *Idiom Book of New Testament Greek,* page 100 urges Acts 25:13 as the sole exception to this last rule, but Robertson refuses to allow even that.

[20] It ought to be noticed how this argument making baptism and circumcision parallel ordinances strengthens the argument drawn from Romans 2:25ff concerning the efficacy of outward ordinances. The greater the parallel, the more what is said of the one applies to the other.

would be unclean, but as it is, they are holy.' In using the words 'unclean' and 'holy' as expressive of mutually exclusive states, Paul is evoking an Old Covenant situation. Numbers 9:6-14 is the most instructive passage for our purpose. Comparison of the opening and closing verses of it shows that there were two possible disqualifications from eating the Passover: uncleanness and uncircumcision. The circumcised could fall into a state of uncleanness, which had to be removed before he could again participate in the great festival of redemption, open only to the holy people. For the heathen man, the bridge over which he could pass from uncleanness to holiness was circumcision (Exodus 12:43-49; cf. Isaiah 35:8; 52:1). In Corinthians, therefore, Paul is urging that the children of even one believing parent are full members of the covenant people of God: they are not unclean; they are holy. But such would be reckoned impossible without the covenant sign, for wilfully to omit the sign is to break the covenant itself (Genesis 17:14). It is hard to see how the inference is to be resisted that Paul was speaking of the baptism of the children of believers.[21]

## 3.4.  *Faith and Baptism*

The entire practice of baptism rests upon the expressed will of God regarding the ordinances of the Covenant of Grace. What he has commanded the Church must do. The faith of the candidate, therefore, is not the ground of baptism. And yet, as we have repeatedly seen, faith and baptism are linked in the New Testament, as were faith and circumcision in the Old (cf. Romans 4:18f). Consequently it is necessary to ask what place faith occupies in respect of the divine command to baptize.

---

[21] Anglicans are often taunted with the fact that the New Testament nowhere describes the baptism of an infant. However, neither does it ever describe the baptism, as an adult believer, of a person who has grown up within the Christian Church. Thus, neither paedo-baptist nor anti-paedo-baptist has a New Testament example of his 'typical' case. Each must proceed upon the discernment of biblical principles.

## 3.5.   *Faith confessed*

In the case of the adult candidate for baptism, his confession of faith is the sign to the church to baptize him. We have followed this out in the practice of the early church in their obedience to the command of the Lord (Acts 8:13; Mark 16:16). Such faith confessed signifies to the church the propriety of baptizing this particular person.

In the case of the infant, the church proceeds upon the confessed faith of the parents. But just as it would be incorrect to say that an adult is baptized 'because of his faith', so we cannot say that a child is baptized 'because of the parents' faith'. A valid baptism is grounded upon the commandment of God, who wills that his church should baptize adults who profess faith in Christ, and also the children of such adults. This faith, so to speak, merely *admits* to baptism, but there is also the faith which *appropriates* baptism. To this we now turn.

## 3.6.   *Appropriating faith*

In adults and children alike, faith is the means whereby the promises of God are personally apprehended and enjoyed. This is a faith consequent upon the outward sign. The Catechism asks: 'What is required of persons to be baptized?' and replies: '...faith, whereby they steadfastly believe the promises of God *made to them in that sacrament.'* Baptism, like circumcision, expresses the covenant promises of God, and these then await the exercise of responsive, appropriating faith on the part of the baptized. The major function of faith in connection with baptism is as a subsequent exercise in appropriation.

## 3.7.   *The state of the baptized*

Consequently, we may say, concerning the condition of a baptized person, that it is one of probation. This is not, of course, how God sees it. God sees not as man sees: man looks upon the outward appearance, but God looks upon the heart. God knows whether any given person is regenerate or not; God knows in whom his Spirit has performed that mighty work. In a word, God alone knows the exact relation between the obedient act of the church and his own secret divine counsel. Once only did he reveal his counsel unmistakably, when he bestowed his Spirit before baptism on Cornelius (Acts 10:44-48), and in that case, therefore, baptism was performed in absolute knowledge of the coincidence of the sign with the thing signified. But in every other case, the church must walk in watchful obedience, while God reserves to himself the knowledge of his own mind. As far as the church is concerned, those who have come in obedience to God's command, the believing adult and the child of believing parents alike, and have been baptized – such persons are in a state of probation.

This may be illustrated by the spiritual situation of a person who makes a profession of conversion at an evangelistic service. The gospel has been preached, and someone professes that he has turned to Christ in repentance and faith. Now, God knows the heart of such a person, and God knows his own mind concerning such a person, for 'the Lord know those who are his'. God knows if in reality that person has passed from darkness to light. But what does the church, represented by the preacher, or the Christian friend, know? The church only knows the outward testimony. Nevertheless, acting towards such a one in a spirit of faith, it is the task of the church to address him in the language of assurance, asserting the promises which God makes to those who trust Christ: You are a member of Christ, a child of God, and an inheritor of the kingdom of heaven. But this is the language of faith, and only the evidence of a transformed life, a daily walk with God, a love of the brethren, an abhorrence of sin, and such things can transform faith into certainty. And these things will follow if the probationer is a genuine believer.

Likewise, in baptism, when in accordance with the command of God, the church baptizes the adult who testifies of his faith or the child of believers, it does not surround him with 'ifs' but with prayers and promises, asserting all that God has pledged in his covenant of grace, and believing that what he has promised 'He for his part will most surely keep and perform'.[22] Because our practice of baptism is not grounded on anything as insecure as man's professed faith, but upon the word of God which lives and abides for ever, we can afford to speak with all the boldness of faith. There is none so secure as he who stands upon the promises of God.

**Editor's Note**: This chapter was originally a Latimer Lecture and was first published in 1962 by the Fellowship of Evangelical Churchmen.

---

[22] The attitude of the Christian parent towards his baptized child is always one of certainty based upon faith. He does not look forward to, nor expect, the 'conversion' of his child, but, believing that God has claimed the child as his own from the very start, the parent prays for, and teaches, and fosters growth in Christian living. Baptism is never an attempt to force God's hand, but is rather a humble submission to his will. He has commanded the baptism of the children of Christian homes. Christian parents will gladly seize upon this token of God's goodwill towards their dear children, and will believe that the promises which God has sealed to each in the covenant ordinance he will in his time and way fulfil.

# LATIMER PUBLICATIONS

LS 01  *The Evangelical Anglican Identity Problem*  Jim Packer

LS 02  *The ASB Rite A Communion: A Way Forward*  Roger Beckwith

LS 03  *The Doctrine of Justification in the Church of England*  Robin Leaver

LS 04  *Justification Today: The Roman Catholic and Anglican Debate*  R. G. England

LS 05/06  *Homosexuals in the Christian Fellowship*  David Atkinson

LS 07  *Nationhood: A Christian Perspective*  O. R. Johnston

LS 08  *Evangelical Anglican Identity: Problems and Prospects*  Tom Wright

LS 09  *Confessing the Faith in the Church of England Today*  Roger Beckwith

LS 10  *A Kind of Noah's Ark? The Anglican Commitment to Comprehensiveness*  Jim Packer

LS 11  *Sickness and Healing in the Church*  Donald Allister

LS 12  *Rome and Reformation Today: How Luther Speaks to the New Situation*  James Atkinson

LS 13  *Music as Preaching: Bach, Passions and Music in Worship*  Robin Leaver

LS 14  *Jesus Through Other Eyes: Christology in a Multi-Faith Context*  Christopher Lamb

LS 15  *Church and State Under God*  James Atkinson

LS 16  *Language and Liturgy*  Gerald Bray, Steve Wilcockson, Robin Leaver

LS 17  *Christianity and Judaism: New Understanding, New Relationship*  James Atkinson

LS 18  *Sacraments and Ministry in Ecumenical Perspective*  Gerald Bray

LS 19  *The Functions of a National Church*  Max Warren

LS 20/21  *The Thirty-Nine Articles: Their Place and Use Today*  Jim Packer, Roger Beckwith

LS 22  *How We Got Our Prayer Book*  T. W. Drury, Roger Beckwith

LS 23/24  *Creation or Evolution: a False Antithesis?*  Mike Poole, Gordon Wenham

LS 25  *Christianity and the Craft*  Gerard Moate

LS 26  *ARCIC II and Justification*  Alister McGrath

LS 27  *The Challenge of the Housechurches*  Tony Higton, Gilbert Kirby

LS 28  *Communion for Children? The Current Debate*  A. A. Langdon

LS 29/30  *Theological Politics*  Nigel Biggar

LS 31  *Eucharistic Consecration in the First Four Centuries and its Implications for Liturgical Reform*  Nigel Scotland

LS 32  *A Christian Theological Language*  Gerald Bray

LS 33  *Mission in Unity: The Bible and Missionary Structures*  Duncan McMann

LS 34  *Stewards of Creation: Environmentalism in the Light of Biblical Teaching*  Lawrence Osborn

LS 35/36  *Mission and Evangelism in Recent Thinking: 1974-1986*  Robert Bashford

LS 37  *Future Patterns of Episcopacy: Reflections in Retirement*  Stuart Blanch

# LATIMER PUBLICATIONS

LS 38   *Christian Character: Jeremy Taylor and Christian Ethics Today*
David Scott

LS 39   *Islam: Towards a Christian Assessment*   Hugh Goddard

LS 40   *Liberal Catholicism: Charles Gore and the Question of Authority*
G. F. Grimes

LS 41/42   *The Christian Message in a Multi-Faith Society*   Colin Chapman

LS 43   *The Way of Holiness 1: Principles*
D. A. Ousley

LS 44/45   *The Lambeth Articles*  V. C. Miller

LS 46   *The Way of Holiness 2: Issues*
D. A. Ousley

LS 47   *Building Multi-Racial Churches*
John Root

LS 48   *Episcopal Oversight: A Case for Reform*   David Holloway

LS 49   *Euthanasia: A Christian Evaluation*   Henk Jochemsen

LS 50/51   *The Rough Places Plain: AEA 1995*

LS 52   *A Critique of Spirituality*
John Pearce

LS 53/54   *The Toronto Blessing*
Martyn Percy

LS 55   *The Theology of Rowan Williams*
Garry Williams

LS 56/57   *Reforming Forwards? The Process of Reception and the Consecration of Woman as Bishops*  Peter Toon

LS 58   *The Oath of Canonical Obedience*
Gerald Bray

LS 59   *The Parish System: The Same Yesterday, Today And For Ever?*
Mark Burkill

LS 60   *'I Absolve You': Private Confession and the Church of England*   Andrew Atherstone

LS 61   *The Water and the Wine: A Contribution to the Debate on Children and Holy Communion*
Roger Beckwith,
Andrew Daunton-Fear

LS 62   *Must God Punish Sin?*
Ben Cooper

LS 63   *Too Big For Words?: The Transcendence of God and Finite Human Speech*
Mark D. Thompson

LS 64   *A Step Too Far: An Evangelical Critique of Christian Mysticism*
Marian Raikes

LS 65   *The New Testament and Slavery: Approaches and Implications*
Mark Meynell

LS 66   *The Tragedy of 1662: The Ejection and Persecution of the Puritans*
Lee Gatiss

LS 67   *Heresy, Schism & Apostasy*
Gerald Bray

LB01   *The Church of England: What it is, and what it stands for*
Roger T. Beckwith

LB02   *Praying with Understanding: Explanations of Words and Passages in the Book of Common Prayer*   Roger T. Beckwith

LB03   *The Failure of the Church of England? The Church, the Nation and the Anglican Communion*
A. Pollard

LB04   *Towards a Heritage Renewed*
H.R.M. Craig

LB05   *Christ's Gospel to the Nations: The Heart & Mind of Evangelicalism Past, Present & Future*   Peter Jensen

## LATIMER PUBLICATIONS

LB06     *Passion for the Gospel: Hugh
Latimer (1485-1555) Then and
Now. A commemorative lecture
to mark the 450$^{th}$ anniversary of
his martyrdom in Oxford*

          A. McGrath

LB07     *Truth and Unity in Christian
Fellowship*     Michael Nazir-Ali


GGC     *God, Gays and the Church:
Human Sexuality and Experience
in Christian Thinking*

          eds. Lisa Nolland, Chris Sugden
& Sarah Finch

GAFCON   *The Way, the Truth and the Life:
Theologcial Resources for a
Pilgrimage to a Global Anglican
Future*

          eds. Vinay Samuel, Chris Sugden,
Sarah Finch